Veterans at Goldman Sachs

~ A Guide to Help Military Veterans Evaluate and Pursue a Career at Goldman Sachs ~

Justin M. Nassiri

Veterans at Goldman Sachs: A Guide to Help Military
Veterans Evaluate and Pursue a Career at Goldman
Sachs

ISBN: 9781980253785

Cover creation by CreativeLog Deisgn

Table of Contents

To my accountant, Camran, who left a life of security and promise to immigrate to the United States in search of a better life. You set the example for me of independence and taking a risk.

I wouldn't be where I am without your measured perspective, advice, and undying support.

Introduction

In the 150+ interviews of U.S. Military Veterans that I have conducted with *Beyond the Uniform*, I have found two things to be true. **The first is that U.S. Military Veterans can do absolutely any civilian career imaginable.** Their military experience and skills honed while in the Armed Forces close no doors, and in many ways uniquely prepares them to pursue an incredibly diverse range of career options. However, the second truth I have observed is that **most Veterans drastically underestimate what it will take to pursue their desired career.**

My intention with this book – as with *Beyond the Uniform* – is to provide U.S. Military Veterans with the information, tools, and advice necessary to identify, pursue, and succeed at their ideal civilian career. If you read this book and decide that a career in Investment Banking or specifically at Goldman Sachs is not a career path you would like to pursue, that is just as much a victory as identifying it as your next career choice. As my career counselor, Andy Chen, told me at the Stanford Graduate School of Business: "Don't worry about finding out what you want to do. Start figuring out what you don't want to do, and start closing those doors."

This book is based on a quantitative analysis of every public LinkedIn profile of U.S. Military Veterans who are currently working at Goldman Sachs. It is also based on over four hours of qualitative interviews with U.S. Military Veterans who have worked at Goldman Sachs. Lastly, it is based on the over 150 hours of interviews I have completed with U.S. Military Veterans about their civilian career. I have combined everything that I know about Goldman Sachs and its compatibility with a U.S. Military Veteran with the hope that it provides you with the knowledge to decide how this career path may align with your unique interests, desires, and skill set.

As Master Chief Granito would always tell us on the USS Alaska: "Knowledge is power." I hope this knowledge takes you one step closer to finding the ideal career that you deserve.

How this Book is Structured

I have structured this book to first cover the more qualitative aspects of Goldman Sachs – why you may like this career, what it is, how that translates to a daily and weekly lifestyle, etc. For this section of the book, I have relied upon the qualitative interviews I have conducted through *Beyond the Uniform*.

The second portion of this book focuses on more quantitative analysis, based on a statistical analysis of public profiles on LinkedIn. My reasoning for this approach to data analysis is that, while few take the time to complete surveys, nearly all professionals in the civilian sector have an updated and accurate LinkedIn profile. Thus, this seems to be the most comprehensive and accurate database of Veteran information available as of the time of this writing.

It is worth noting that my intention for providing this data is simply to inform. In the 150+ interviews I have conducted for *Beyond the Uniform*, I have seen that there is no single path to any career destination. Veterans are capable of forging their own way and setting their own path. However, I do believe it is valuable to at least understand that path that many other Veterans have taken in pursuing a career at Goldman Sachs. So, I hope that this information is helpful – but not limiting – in your consideration of a career at Goldman Sachs.

Methodology

I based my LinkedIn analysis on all public LinkedIn profiles in January of 2018 who were currently working at Goldman Sachs and had a "Previous Company" listed as either the U.S. Army, U.S. Air Force, U.S. Coast Guard, U.S. Marine Corps, or U.S. Navy. In the second part of this book, where appropriate, I will mention any special consideration for a particular analysis.

One downside in using LinkedIn as the foundation of my research is that some Veterans (particularly those who are more senior at Goldman Sachs) do not provide much insight into their career path. For example, one may list on LinkedIn their current title as Managing Director, and that they have been in this role for fifteen years. The truth is that they have worked their way up to this position, but for research purposes, I only have access to this final role. However, Goldman Sachs (and Investment Banking in general) are relatively stratified organizations, so it is possible to tease out the typical career path even with these irregularities.

All salary information provided was based on Glassdoor.com's Total Compensation, which combines Base Pay and Additional Pay for each respective title. I used New York as the location for all job titles researched on GlassDoor. I did this to keep the different salaries as comparable as possible, and because New York is the headquarters of Goldman Sachs. In the rare case that a job title was not available in New York (e.g. Goldman Sachs Private Wealth Advisor), I used San Francisco instead of New York. At the time of writing, the pay scale and cost of living is likely very equivalent in these two locations. While New York may represent the higher end of the Goldman Sachs pay scale, it is also the epicenter of banking.

Who I Interviewed for this Book

I refer frequently to conversations with a few people, and I would like to give you their background upfront so you can factor that in to the advice they provide. Here are the people I will reference in this book:

- **Matthew Caldwell** is the President and CEO of the Florida Panthers and Sunrise Sports & Entertainment. Matthew started out at West Point, after which he served in the U.S. Army for five years, conducting combat operations in Iraq and peacekeeping operations in Kosovo. Matthew worked as a Vice President at Goldman Sachs in their Investment Management Division, and then transitioned to Chief Operating Officer for the Panthers before being elevated to President and CEO. Matthew holds a JD/MBA from Northwestern University School of Law and the Kellogg School of Management.

- **Chris Dattaro** is an Operations Manager at Lyft in Washington DC. He started out at the Naval Academy, after which he served as a Surface Warfare Officer for five years. After departing the Navy, Chris participated in the Goldman Sachs 3 month Veterans Integration Program, before joining FBR, an investment bank, in an Institutional Equity Sales role.

- **Lee Haney** works in Business Operations & Strategy for the COO of Hewlett Packard Enterprise. He graduated in the top 5% of his class at the Naval Academy, and served in the Marine Corps for five years as a Human intelligence Officer, with deployments to both Iraq and Afghanistan. After transitioning out of the military, Lee attended the University of Chicago's Booth School of Business, where he graduated with honors. Since getting his MBA, Lee has worked in the Finance Industry with Goldman Sachs as an Investment Banking Associate, before transitioning to HPE.

- **Andrew Neuwirth** is a Private Wealth Advisor at Goldman Sachs. He started out at the Naval Academy, after which he served as a Submarine

Officer for seven years. After his military service, he transitioned directly to Goldman Sachs.

Why Goldman Sachs?

In 2016, I analyzed over 5000 LinkedIn profiles of U.S. Military Veterans to determine trends in what this population does after their military service. As far as I know, it is the first research of its kind. One thing I realized during this process is that **Financial Service is the 4th largest industry that members of the Armed Forces enter into after their military service.**

Given how many Veterans enter into this space, I wanted to start my research by looking at one representative company. I selected Goldman Sachs due to their exceptional reputation both for the quality of their work as well as the difficulty of their interview process. When I was at the Stanford Graduate School of Business, Goldman Sachs was widely considered amongst the most difficult to obtain jobs. By providing an overview of life at Goldman Sachs, as well as the type of Veteran who works there, I intend to give a glimpse of what it takes to compete at the pinnacle of an industry.

It goes without saying that Financial Services is a massive and widely varying industry. That said, a foundational understanding of how Veterans fit in at one of the most respected firms in this sector will provide clarity for subsequent career searches.

Next, we'll do a quick overview of what exactly
Goldman Sachs is before we dive into the particulars of
what life is like there.

What is Goldman Sachs?

Most Veterans are probably familiar with Goldman
Sachs by name, but perhaps not much more beyond that.
That was Lee Haney's experience, as he explains:

> "My initial impression of Goldman Sachs is
> probably similar to many people, and that's just
> having heard their name growing up. I pictured a
> big trading floor with people yelling and
> screaming, papers flying around, and phones
> being banged on the desk. But going in and
> seeing how much variety there is in terms of
> what the institution does was really sobering for
> me to understand the bigger picture. At the end
> of the day, while Goldman Sachs may not have
> branches out on the street or ATM machines, it is
> still a bank in the sense that it is trying to help
> people who have money either save it and try to
> invest it in a way that is going to grow their
> portfolio, which is their Sales & Trading effort.
> Or they are advising people and specifically large
> companies on how they are going to make
> strategic decisions that would require lots of
> capital – lots of money to invest to either
> organically grow their businesses, or acquire
> other businesses."

I appreciate Lee's simplistic explanation for what is the
fifth largest bank in the United States by total assets
($930B), a company that does over $37.7 Billion in

revenue each year, and has over 33,000 employees at over 80 locations in 28 different locations.

Matthew Caldwell summarized Goldman's 149-year history by saying:

> "It is a great firm – over many generations they've produced great people who have done great things for the country."

It's even more difficult to explain what Goldman Sachs employees do, as there are so many different types of employees. Fortunately, however, as we'll see in the second part of this book, there is a high level of consistency in the titles that Veterans find within Goldman. Here is how Lee Haney explained the type of work that people do at Goldman Sachs:

> "If I were to think of a role that is similar in the military to something that represents the entirety of Goldman Sachs, it doesn't exist. But in terms of Investment Banking specifically, it's really to serve as a trusted advisor to help make major decisions. So, for someone who has been around for a while and seen a number of major military operations in the past and is able to advise the Commanding General on how a major operation should take place, I think that's really what Investment Bankers do. They help people make this big, life-or-death decisions for companies that they may not have lived through once themselves before."

Although Andrew Neuwirth, as a Private Wealth Advisor at Goldman, has a very different role than Lee had, he described his experience very similarly:

> "What is so interesting about this role is that you're a trusted advisor. When a big decision gets made, you're the first call. When I was on submarines and on watch, others in the crew would call me and say, 'Can we do this? Can this work?'. You would then run through your decision-making process and then move forward. It's similar in my current role. The infrastructure at Goldman supports us in a way that allows us to interact with the best strategists and the best thinkers so that we can provide risk control to our clients. These are the most important families and business leaders in the world who rely on us to protect and mitigate that management risk."

Matthew Caldwell, who as a Vice President at Goldman Sachs in their Investment Management Division was the most senior Veteran I interviewed, told a similar story about his daily life:

> "In my everyday life [at Goldman] I worked on a team with about six individuals managing thirty or so accounts: big families, foundations, non-profit, another company's assets, etc. We were the intermediary between the client – what are their needs, what are they trying to do – and then we would sit with all the experts at the firm (in research, or investing in Europe, or Latin

America, etc). We'd be the intermediary between them and the resources at Goldman. A lot of my job was listening to my clients, hearing their needs, running around and talking to different departments and then making recommendations."

Just as Andrew described how this related to his work on submarines, I hope that Matthew's description illustrates how similar this career path is to the military. While there is a vast difference in the terminology, tactical skills, and industry expertise required at Goldman Sachs, the underlying premise of the work is not entirely related to many Veterans' military experience.

One other aspect that I found interesting was how each of these Veterans ended up at Goldman Sachs. None of them had premediated heavily on working at Goldman Sachs, or the finance industry in general. Each of their stories had some amount of serendipity as far as how they ended up at Goldman.

Chris Dattaro shared his story of how he initially found his way to Goldman:

> "I had always had an interest in finance; I was an economics major. I thought that having a background in finance can be applicable to any vertical or job industry. So, I made Finance my focus. A former Lacrosse teammate of mine told me about the Veterans Integration Program at Goldman. So, I went through the interview process and was lucky enough to be selected."

The Veterans Integration Program is a common route for Veterans, and one that we will explore in more detail when we talk about Applications.

Now that we've covered some background information about Goldman Sachs, let's take a look at early signs that you may love (or hate) a career at Goldman Sachs.

Why Veterans May Love (or Hate) Life at Goldman Sachs

When I was on Active Duty, I had little (if any) idea about what I wanted to do in my civilian career. As a result, I'm always eager to ask Veterans to point out signs that another Veteran may love his/her new career. It's also helpful to know the indications that they may hate that career as well. While nothing beats some hands-on experience, my intention in asking this is to help Veterans identify – or rule out – a potential career as quickly as possible.

Chris Dattaro was exuberant about his experience at Goldman Sachs, and why other Veterans should consider this as their first career move, even if it is not their long-term career aspiration. As he shared:

> "In my opinion, [Goldman Sachs] is one of the best things that you can do when you get out of the military. Especially if you have an interest in finance, but even if you do not. Goldman Sachs is a great institution: they have a very strong Veterans network and it's a very strong brand. Even if you do not stay at Goldman long-term (as I did not), it's great to have their brand on your resume and their network."

Given that Chris ultimately did not stay at Goldman Sachs after his internship, I find his advice particularly relevant. Many of the Veterans I interview for Beyond the Uniform talk about how they approached their first career thinking that it would be their long-term career as well. This is rarely the case. From that vantage point, starting one's career at Goldman Sachs can be beneficial regardless of what path you take after your tenure.

Each of the people I interviewed spoke to the incredible talent that they worked with while at Goldman. Given how difficult it is to obtain a job there, it makes sense that the average employee is an exceptionally high caliber professional. This is what Lee Haney found to be true:

> "The best part of my experience (and this may sound a bit like a cliché) was the people. Despite what I may have thought from my initial Main Street perspective, and despite what people may see on the news or on TV, I thought I found the nicest people I'd ever come across while at Goldman Sachs. These are people I still want to spend time with on the weekends, and they're the type of people I would trust with my kids when I have kids someday. That's something that, while maybe not expected, is the best part I think of when I think of my time at Goldman."

As a Veteran establishes their professional network, the value of these connections cannot be overstated. It's great that Lee had such great report with his colleagues, but his colleagues' abilities matter just as much. Even if you only work at Goldman for a few years, you are part of their alumni network, which can open up doors for the rest of one's career.

One of the most commonly cited downsides to a career at Goldman Sachs is the extremely demanding schedule. We'll get to that in a moment, but first I wanted to highlight one benefit of that grueling schedule. Several of the Veterans I interviewed spoke to how they felt as if they received two years of experience in just one year. For someone transitioning directly from the military, this rapid "catch-up" period can be very advantageous. As Lee Haney put it:

> "Strategically, I don't' think I would be anywhere near where I am today without having had that experience. Both because of where you can go after an experience like Goldman Sachs, and also because of the skills I was able to build there in a pretty short period of time. I really think that's been important for my success after Goldman."

The downsides of working at Goldman Sachs was the same across the board: the lifestyle. Goldman Sachs (and Investment Banking in general) has a reputation for hundred-hour workweeks. While this, at times, may be true, the people I interviewed spoke to something beyond that. Here's how Lee Haney put it:

"In terms of the challenges, I don't think anyone is surprised by the challenges or how difficult it is to work through the long hours. But I think it's much less about the shear duration and more just about the uncertainty. I think that pretty much everyone could manage working through three extremely long days at work where you're getting very little sleep. But what's much harder is telling your wife five minutes after you're already supposed to be at home that you're going to be late, and that you're going to be arriving four hours after you thought you would be home. I think that those surprises for when you lose your free time are some of the harder things to deal with. I do think this is part of what's changing in the industry. Maybe the full number of hours doesn't change much, but giving someone an entire Saturday where they know they can make plans with friends really serves to lessen that impact. I think when bankers talk about their long hours, they're not meaning the number of hours it's really more the uncertainty that you get.

It is worth noting, as Lee points out, that the Finance industry in general appears to be making changes to make their schedule more palatable. But this is certainly something to ask about as you meet with people currently at Goldman Sachs to see if it matches your career and personal intentions.

One last piece of advice given that I wanted to share was an aside that Lee Haney shared with me:

> "It is very challenging to get into Investment Banking – it's extremely competitive. One indicator that you should keep in mind is how comfortable you feel with math at a very basic level. If you like math and enjoy spending a lot of time with numbers, this could be a path that you would really enjoy doing day-in and day-out. If you can't imagine yourself wanting to solve math problems at 2:00 or 3:00 AM, that also may be an indicator."

That may be the most succinct explanation I've heard to help Veterans have an initial sense of whether or not this career path is compatible with their desires.

Now that we've cleared an initial hurdle about an interest in Goldman Sachs, let's zoom in and look at what a day at Goldman Sachs looks like.

Hours & Lifestyle

When I speak with Veterans about their civilian career, there tends to be three areas of concern for them. The first is the number of hours that they will need to work each week in their new role. The second is the amount of travel that a job will entail and how this may impact their weekends. And the third is their overall work-life balance. These are all important aspects to consider when evaluating any career.

As a result, the next aspect I asked about in my interviews was getting a sense of what day-to-day life is like at Goldman Sachs.

Andrew Neuwirth took me through his typical day as a Private Wealth Advisor in San Francisco:

> "Because I work on the West Coast but markets open on the East Coast, we get to the office pretty early. I try to be here right around 6 a.m. The first part of my day is to gain an understanding of what happened overnight and what might happen during the day. I read the Wall Street Journal and other news sources to gain that picture. Goldman also has a massive research arm that puts out probably more information than you could read in a 24-hour period. I try to highlight a few of every single day. Being aware of the news is important

24

because it structures the conversation throughout the day.

I've been here for about two years and I'm on a team with four total advisors. We all manage a number of clients and what we refer to as a "Book of Business". These clients have a direct relationship with one of the advisors. I help them cover these clients. And then for me, these advisors serve as my team as a I go out and meet potential clients for the firm. Part of my role is to build and form relationships and bring folks into the firm. That could be going out and meeting people in person or through a phone call."

Lee Haney provided the most exhaustive description of his daily routine. As an Associate, or entry-level Investment Banking position, he broke each down into two parts, what he called a Day A and a Day B. Here's what he shared:

"Much like being deployed, each day as an Associate can be a bit different. On the whole, it reminded me very much of being deployed, with the clear exceptions of a complete lack of danger and the fact that I could take a shower at the end of each day. But otherwise, I felt that there was this very strong sense of comradery with the people you're working with, because you're all working very, very hard. And you're potentially working quite long hours. In terms of the day-today experience, it was hard for me to imagine what 100-hour workweek looked like in practice.

If I could break the day into two parts, I would say there is a Day A and a Day B. Day A was usually 9:00 AM to 5:00 PM, and could be filled with meetings from start to finish, or it could include walking around and having coffee chats with people who are interested in the company, or getting to know other people who are working in the firm.

Day B was after dinner time, when you really started to get down and do the work and the analysis. It reminded me a lot of being in the military and being out on patrol and still having a lot of work to do after that to get ready for the next day. In that sense, it was a very comfortable environment, because you may not know what the work itself will be the next day, but I was very comfortable with the type of uncertainty that was going on.

If in the course of Day A you're in meetings all day or talking to clients, Day B was following up on any questions or requests that happened during Day A. That would be working with a financial model to build out what you'd expect you'd need to present on the next day in terms of the valuation of a company. Or it could be answering specific questions that someone or maybe even the client had about something. That's where a lot of those technical skills that people talk about for finance, that's where those are really utilized most heavily. And so, there is a lot of time on PowerPoint and Excel in the evenings, getting ready for the next day to be presenting those findings to people."

Many Active Duty military personnel have written me at Beyond the Uniform with questions and concerns related to their eventual civilian career's work/life balance. I believe that Lee's answer is very representative of the long hours required from most roles at Goldman Sachs. That said, Andrew Neuwirth had this to say about work/life balance:

"It's a constant topic of conversation and work/life balance is extremely important. Goldman is great for that in allowing their people to do what they need to do to maintain that balance. With that being said we are in the business of helping our clients make money. That's not something that can be done with a lackadaisical approach. How I think about work/life balance is that I try to keep both my family and my work sacred. And there's not a black and white line. It's a constant conversation and you're always iterating on that and what it means to have that balance."

This is consistent with many of the interviews I've had with Veterans at The Big Three management consulting companies (McKinsey & Company, Bain & Company, and The Boston Consulting Group). These are also companies that have reputations for demanding work schedules. However, they also seem to be similar to Goldman Sachs in that you can have some input in what time is sacred and what boundaries you set.

One last aspect I would like to cover here is another way of looking at the extreme workload a Veteran will have at Goldman Sachs. An hundred-hour work week is pretty crazy – that's 14 hour days, 7 days a week. However, I appreciate the perspective that Lee Haney shared, about how this crucible experience of 100 hours a week doing financial analysis and excel work will get you very good very quickly. Your technical skills and tactical abilities ramp up rapidly. As he put it:

> "That's what drew me to Goldman Sachs after going through one internship, and made me want to come back. If you're going to be working that many hours that's how many hours you're going to be learning too. So, in the course of one year of working in Investment Banking, you're effectively getting two years of experience that you would have gotten working somewhere else in terms of the shear amount of time you're exposed to thinking about these key business problems. I think that many people can commiserate about the idea of the longest week

at an 40-hour workweek job, could potentially feel longer than an 100 hour week in an intense job if you're just sitting around and waiting for the next thing to come up. I felt like I was always highly intellectually engaged in those 100 hours. I always felt like I was learning, and wasn't necessarily that I was being driven so hard that it was unsustainable."

If you're not scared off of applying to Goldman Sachs, let's next consider what the application process is like.

Applying

In the second half of this book we'll look at specific data around the most common routes that Veterans take to Goldman Sachs. However, the data matched much of what I learned in my interviews.

When I asked Andrew Neuwirth about the most common paths for a Veteran to get into Goldman Sachs, he told me:

> "Certainly, business school and the Veterans Integration Program. I've also seen people go into financial services after the military and end up moving laterally into Goldman Sachs. Those are really the main paths I've seen."

Of each of these three options, the one that came up most consistently was the Veterans Integration Program. In fact, while each of the people I interviewed had advice to share with Veterans about how to apply for at Goldman Sachs, the most consistent and emphatic recommendation was: **learn about the Veterans Integration Program**.

Here is how Lee Haney described the Veterans Integration Program:

> "The Veterans Integration Program is setup for any veterans transitioning to a civilian career. In my opinion, it is the best possible transition

program someone could go through who is interested in finance. It's for people who are not only doing Investment Banking, but there are also Operations roles, Risk Management roles, and a variety of other positions available. Think of every MOS or Warfare Specialty you could have, you have that same variety of options available at Goldman to try out for about two months in the Spring."

One aspect that strikes me appealing about the Veterans Integration Program is this broad exposure that Lee describes. Rather than taking two years in an MBA program, a Veteran is able to quickly get the lay of the land and understand if they would enjoy a career at Goldman Sachs or in finance in general. Andrew Neuwirth added his experience:

"Goldman Sachs started the program I think six years ago. I was the fifth class to go through. At its most basic level, it's a 8-10 week internship for recently transitioned members of the armed forces to learn more about the financial services industry. The way that I think about it now having gone through the program is that it's basically an MBA internship. It's a little bit off cycle but similar in nature. We had the same access to programs and information that the MBA students had. I was fortunate enough to have the opportunity to learn that it was something that I really wanted to do and there

happened to be a seat open for me which I was
able to successfully move into."

Andrew's experience showed me that a Veteran can
obtain extremely specialized knowledge in a short
amount of time.

Chris Dattaro spoke to the extremely rigorous nature of
the Veterans Integration Program, and how many
Veterans enter this program just days after completing
their military service:

> "My first week [of the Veterans Integration
> Program] was orientation. For myself and many
> other Veterans, we left Active Duty on a Friday,
> packed up our stuff and moved over the
> weekend, and went to Goldman Sachs on
> Monday in a suit and a tie. The transition was
> pretty drastic. That first week was mostly about
> getting integrated and meeting some very high-
> level people at the bank, as well as a quick crash
> course in Microsoft Excel. The next eight or nine
> weeks we were assigned to a specific team and it
> was a two-way job interview. You live that life
> and decide whether that is interesting to you, and
> the team decides if they'd like to offer you a full-
> time offer."

From this perspective, the Veterans Integration Program
seems like an ideal way for a Veteran to evaluate a
career in the Finance industry. Over the course of eight
weeks, you receive exposure to multiple facets of the

finance world and get to understand if this is a suitable career for you. This starts with the initial process of the Veterans Integration Program, where you start to choose what career paths you'd like to explore at Goldman. As Andrew explained:

> "In the initial application phase, you select up to three roles within the firm's different business lines. I only selected the advisory role within investment management. I was confident that if I went into finance, that was the role that I wanted to have. But I've had colleagues that interviewed for a number of different roles.
>
> A brief summary of some of the other roles are, first, an Investment Banking Associate. The Associate joins a team focused on a specific sector or sub-sector. That team helps with everything that the Investment Bank does. Things such as issuances and underwriting. There are also positions within operations and technology, those work as the middle or back office of the firm. They are the true guts of the firm. Without those people, this place would collapse. These people manage everything from making sure our internet is secure to making sure the exchange where we make trades is operating properly."

While Andrew knew right away that he wanted to go into the Private Wealth Advisor group, Chris Dattaro selected another route. As he explains his role:

"I was assigned to a team called "US Institutional Distribution," which was under the Investment Management Division. Their main product was selling Goldman products and strategies to very large pension plans (like Ford Motor Company or municipal governments who have very large requirements for retirement for their employees). These pension plans are looking to invest, and part of our job was to obtain these organizations as clients."

For Veterans who are uncertain of which group would be the most ideal for their interests, there's no need to stress. It seems like the Veterans Integration Program is structure similarly to a traditional college internship program. For those who went to a Service Academy, Andrew explained his perspective this way:

"When we were at the Naval Academy and did different experiences during the summer, the men and women that we interacted with on boats, submarines, etc. were committed to giving us honest and supportive feedback. That's similar to what happened during the Veterans Integration Program. From the most senior to the most junior, everyone here made themselves available for everyone in the program."

I love this perspective that the goal of the Veterans Integration Program is to find the right fit on both sides. So, on the one hand this is a Veteran is being evaluated on their performance and fit within Goldman Sachs. On the other hand, the Veteran is meeting and working with a variety of different employees at Goldman Sachs to help figure out if this is a good fit for their aspirations. I respect that the Goldman team is both accessible and honest in their feedback about their own experience within the firm. After all, if someone decides to join under a poor understanding of the actuality of the culture and work environment, neither the Veteran or Goldman Sachs are benefited.

This is another advantage of the Veterans Integration Program is that you do not need to commit to working at Goldman Sachs to go through it. Although, Andrew did caveat this that:

> "There were folks who were going off to do their MBA afterwards, but for the most part the lion's share of participants were directly making their transition from the military and looking for fulltime employment."

One particular example of an exception to this is Chris Dattaro, who completed the Veterans Integration Program and went on to work at a different Investment Bank. When Chris went through the Veteran Integration Program in New York, his wife was still serving on Active Duty in the Washington D.C. area. After the three-month internship, he returned to Washington D.C. and found a job in finance there.

It's worth noting that acceptance into the Veterans Integration Program is not acceptance into Goldman Sachs. Andrew shared this with me:

> "I think there were six people in my cohort in the investment management division. Five out of those six ended up at Goldman working full-time. The sixth went to business school. With the other folks in the cohort, I think most people were successful in gaining full-time employment at Goldman if they wanted that."

So, while it is likely that you will receive an opportunity for full-time employment, it is by no means guaranteed.

The Veterans Integration Program is by no means the only way to gain admittance to Goldman Sachs. Most of the Veterans I interviewed spoke to the importance of networking. As Matthew Caldwell told me:

> "I looked at and knew that I wanted to go to business. While there I really enjoyed the finance classes, and that helped me determine what sort of I wanted to be most associated with. I did an exhaustive search and talked to consulting companies, as well as larger corporations like General Electric and Proctor and Gamble. But I felt like I connected with the people in the finance industry the most. They were diverse, hardworking, and I wanted to be in an environment like that."

Lee Haney also mentioned that his experience networking with Goldman Sachs employees was ultimately what led him to apply:

> "As I started to learn more about Goldman Sachs in particular, I started to feel a draw – not to the exact work application of Investment Banking – but really the people and the environment. I felt like it would be a place where I would be surrounded by not only people who were extremely hard workers and very intelligent. The folks whom I met in the interview process and Veterans I was able to connect with before starting work there, I really felt like I would be at home. Not only could I learn from them, but they are the type of people I would want to be my next-door neighbors and watch my kids someday. And growing up on Main Street and not having any exposure to Wall Street, I didn't ever expect that to be the case. So, it was really a personal draw to the people and the environment. I thought I could learn and prosper intellectually in a place where I'm comfortable with everyone around me and know they have my best interest at heart."

Regardless of whether you pursue a career at Goldman Sachs or elsewhere, there is an extreme value in networking. By getting to know other Veterans or people at a given company or industry, it makes it easier to assess whether you would be happy there too.

Before we move on to interviewing, I did want to share one story from a Veteran I interviewed who transitioned to Goldman Sachs from business school. Even though he was at business school, he still had to work hard to network and make his career opportunity. His story shares a message of encouragement, but also demonstrates the value of tenacity and persistence in networking. Here is Matthew Caldwell's story:

"The banks or any firms on Wall Street generally like military Veterans. They appreciate the tenacity, the hard work, the comradery – the characteristics of many service men and women. You put the organization first. The company is more important than the individual. That's not common everywhere. A place like Goldman really values that. It is a tough firm to get into – they usually only hire right out of college or an MBA or other graduate program. They value talent and intelligence and very diverse backgrounds.

If you have an interesting story and they think you can add a lot of value at the firm, they know they can teach you all the finance technique. It's just a matter of hustling to get in front of the right people. I've gone through a job search a lot of times – it's a matter of reading and talking to the right person. Sometimes you do 20 coffee chats and you don't feel like you're making any progress, and then the 21st meeting and it's the perfect meeting. But if you didn't go through all the reps before that you don't know how it would have worked out.

For example, while I was at Business School I took a trip to New York. I sat at Starbucks all day emailing people and calling them and I figured since I was in New York I might as well try to meet with people. For the first few hours I wasn't able to get any response. But after the fortieth or fiftieth email, I was able to connect with someone who was at Credit Suisse who had also gone to West Point. He had a few minutes available and I sat down with him. I was open and honest that Goldman was my first choice, and he introduced me to someone at Goldman. Thirty interviews later I got a job there."

I love this story of persistence, and continuing to reach out to new people to get into whatever company you set your sites on. Now that we've looked at a few ways to "get your foot in the door" at Goldman Sachs, the next step is to start preparing for the interview process. We'll look at this in the next chapter.

.

Interviewing

For such a highly demanding career option, you can imagine how difficult the interview process is. Not to worry – countless Veterans have gone before you and demonstrated that this can be done – it just takes a bit of preparation.

One of the biggest pieces of advice for applying to Goldman Sachs – to network like crazy – was also one of the most consistent pieces of advice about preparing for the interview. Lee Haney shared:

> "What got me set off on this path was my roommate putting me in contact with another Veteran at Goldman Sachs. That led me to what made the biggest difference in my application: talking to a ton of folks who could tell me about their experiences. Everyone lives through it in a slightly different way and so I think hearing it a number of times helped reinforce what would resonate for me versus what was just a different experience for someone ese. And then, keying in on the important things I'd need to be prepared for in interviews. Being ready to present the best version possible of myself come interview day.

> At Goldman in particular, though I believe it is the case for most Investment Banks, there are Veterans everywhere. I advise you to get in touch with every last Veteran your hands on, and

through that you'll probably be introduced to more people as well. Ask those key questions that you couldn't find out from the website otherwise."

By talking with Veterans and other employees at Goldman Sachs, you are able to get a better sense of what it is like to work at Goldman. You'll also be able to gain a lot more detail about working at Goldman than you would be reading their website. This can help you stand out in an interview, because the interviewer will know that you've done your homework. You'll be able to speak – with great specificity – to the type of work that most interests you. You'll be able to ask more probing questions about the interviewer's own experience at Goldman. And you'll be able to convince the interviewer that a career at Goldman Sachs is your main pursuit rather than just a passing interest.

Andrew summarized some fantastic advice about preparing for your interview. He started by explaining a bit more about his experience interviewing:

> "It was a long day. There were about six separate interviews. You could face potentially even more if you are interviewing in different divisions [besides just a single division like I applied to]. It's hard because you know what you did in the military but you only have about 25 minutes to distill that experience and deliver it in an impactful way that translates to the interviewer. You might assume that the person interviewing

you knows what it's like to be on a submarine or be an F18 pilot. But they don't actually know so it's your job to teach them.

The second thing is that you have to learn about what it is you're interviewing for you how you can relate to that. In my case, I talked to as many people at Goldman that were in this role as I could. I tried to stay up to date on anything happening in finance. When I was interviewing, the price of oil was changing and there was a lot going on in China. This was truly interesting to me and it was also something I could bring up in my interview to show that I was genuinely interested in this field."

The importance of storytelling in an interview has come across in most of my 150 Beyond the Uniform interviews. Given the short 25-minute period you have to tell your story, you need to be well-rehearsed and succinct in your explanations. And Andrew's other advice underscores the importance of doing your homework prior to the interview by connecting with as many people at Goldman Sachs as possible.

Over the last several chapters, we've taken a look at the ins-and-outs of what it's like to work at Goldman Sachs, as well as how to get and prepare for your interview. In the remaining chapters, we'll now shift gears and start to take a look at the quantitative side of Goldman Sachs and the Veterans who pursue a career at this company.

What Type of Veteran Works at Goldman Sachs

To better understand how and where military Veterans work at Goldman Sachs, I analyzed LinkedIn profiles of Veterans who are currently working at Goldman Sachs. The following analysis is intended to provide a snapshot of the current working environment at Goldman Sachs. However, if I've learned anything from the 150+ interviews I've done with Beyond the Uniform, it is that there is no one path to a career. So please take these numbers as merely information and trends, and know that you can always forge your own, unpaved way as well.

Branches of military service represented at Goldman Sachs

The first thing to look at is the branches of the Armed Forces currently represented at Goldman Sachs. Bear in mind that for this, and subsequent analysis, this is merely a snapshot at one point of time and that this will certainly vary from time-to-time.

Veterans at Goldman Sachs by Branch of Military Service

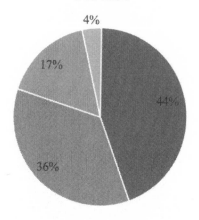

4%

17%

44%

36%

■ Army   ■ Navy   ■ Air Force   ■ Marine Corps   ■ Coast Guard

Figure 1 – The Army is most represented at Goldman Sachs, followed by the Navy, Air Force, and the Marine Corps. The Coast Guard is currently not represented.
(For a color version of this chart, please visit BeyondTheUniform.io/goldman-charts)

The Army is most heavily represented at Goldman Sachs, followed by the Navy. The Air Force comprises a distant third. Based on the relatively smaller population size of the Marine Corps, it's no surprise that they end up fourth. I was unable to find a Coast Guard Alumnus currently working at Goldman Sachs.

Of all the data analyzed, it's my personal opinion that this data should have the least impact on your evaluation of a career at Goldman Sachs. Each branch of the military is well represented at every career path I have studied with Beyond the Uniform, and an underrepresentation of your particular branch of service should not dissuade you from applying and pursuing this sort of career.

Routes that Veterans take from the military to Goldman Sachs

Next, I was curious about the way in which Veterans made their way to Goldman Sachs. To look at this, I categorized the route taken into one of three paths:

1. **School** – the Veteran attended an undergraduate or graduate school program immediately preceding their joining Goldman Sachs.
2. **Direct** – the Veteran went directly from military service to Goldman Sachs.
3. **Industry** – the Veteran worked at another civilian company prior to joining Goldman Sachs. This could be at another Financial Services company or a company in an entirely different industry.

Please note that I only considered what the Veteran was doing **immediately** prior to starting at Goldman Sachs. For example, if a Veteran went from Active Duty into an industry, then went to a school, and then to Goldman Sachs, I still classified their route as "School." Similarly, if a Veteran went to school, then to a job, and then to Goldman Sachs, their route would be classified as "Industry."

Here's what I found:

Veterans by Route Taken to Goldman Sachs

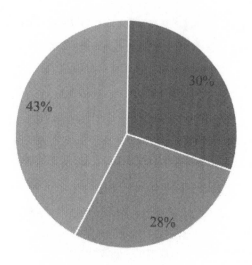

■ Direct ■ School ■ Industry

Figure 2 – Most Veterans at Goldman Sachs work at another
company immediately prior to starting at Goldman Sachs
(For a color version of this chart, please visit
BeyondTheUniform.io/goldman-charts)

When I completed a similar analysis in my book,
Veterans in Consulting, I found that 84% of Veterans at
a Top Three Consulting firm go directly from school to
their job. However, for Veterans at Goldman Sachs the
paths represented are fairly equivocal. The majority of
Veterans leave Active Duty and have some civilian work
experience prior to starting at Goldman Sachs. It is next

most common for a Veteran to go directly from Active Duty to working at Goldman Sachs. I hope that this gives readers some encouragement: one does not necessarily need significant experience or an intermediary academic experience to make the way to this highly-prized employer. And the least likely path (though still 28% of all LinkedIn profiles analyzed) was going to some academic institution prior to Goldman Sachs.

In subsequent sections, we will delve deeper into each of these three options. However, I did want to provide some insight into how this varies based on the branch of service in which the Veteran served.

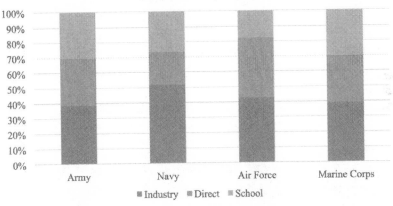

Figure 3 – A look at how branch of military service affects the route that a Veteran takes to Goldman Sachs
(For a color version of this chart, please visit BeyondTheUniform.io/goldman-charts)

Of all the branches of service, Air Force Veterans are the most likely to transition directly from the Active Duty to Goldman Sachs. Navy Veterans are the most likely to work in another civilian job prior to joining Goldman Sachs. And the Army and Marine Corps are tied for their propensity to attend an academic institution immediately prior to joining Goldman Sachs.

I also found it interesting that Navy Veterans are the least likely to make the direct transition from Active Duty to Goldman Sachs (just **22%** are able to do so). Similarly, Air Force Veterans are the least likely to go to school directly prior to joining Goldman Sachs (just **18%** do so).

It is my opinion that the presence of the Veterans Integration Program minimizes the need of School as a route to Goldman Sachs. Business School in particular plays a much more significant role in a Veterans career path in Management Consulting than it does at Goldman Sachs. If I were on Active Duty and interested in Goldman Sachs, this would give me a lot of confidence. Not only does it save you time in your transition, but it also saves you a significant financial investment.

Duration of Military Service for Veterans at Goldman Sachs

Next, I wanted to see how long Veterans served in the military prior to joining Goldman Sachs.

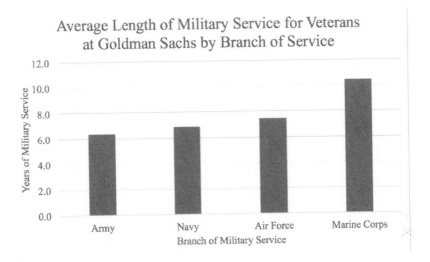

Average Length of Military Service for Veterans at Goldman Sachs by Branch of Service

Figure 4 – Most Veterans at Goldman Sachs have served between six to eight years in the military, with Marines being one the exception.

Across all branches of service, the average Veteran served in the military for **6.9** years prior to joining Goldman Sachs. This seemed to indicate that most Veterans served for their initial 4-5-year commitment as well as a follow-up "shore tour." It is also clear that most Veterans at Goldman Sachs exited the military early in their career.

Intuitively, this makes sense to me. First of all, a career at Goldman Sachs is a significant departure from a traditional military career path. As a result, it makes sense that one would not require as much "career capital" from the military to make the transition. Second, given the reputation that Goldman Sachs has for the intensity of their work, it also makes sense that this would be appealing to those younger in their career.

Let's next consider how the duration of one's military service varies based on the path that a Veteran takes to get to Goldman Sachs.

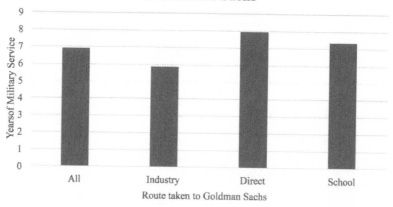

Figure 5 – Veterans who transition directly from the military to Goldman Sachs serve longer on average than those who work in industry or go to an academic institution first.

While the average Veteran at Goldman Sachs has served on Active Duty for **6.9** years, there were trends in each of the paths that Veterans take to get there. For Veterans who work in industry prior to working at Goldman, on average they serve on Active Duty 15% less time than the average Veteran at Goldman Sachs. Similarly, for

Veterans who go directly from Active Duty to Goldman Sachs, on average they serve for 15% longer than the average Veteran at Goldman Sachs. And for those Veterans who go to an academic institution prior to Goldman, on average they serve 7% longer than your average Veteran.

Duration of civilian work experience Veterans obtain prior to Goldman Sachs

After considering the duration of military service, it made sense to look at how long Veterans work in another civilian job capacity prior to joining Goldman. For this aspect, I only considered the amount of civilian work experience for Veterans who went directly to Goldman from industry. So the numbers below are not a reflection of those who went to school first. Obviously, it also ignores those who went directly to Goldman from Active Duty, as this segment does not have any civilian work experience prior to working at Goldman.

Here's what I found:

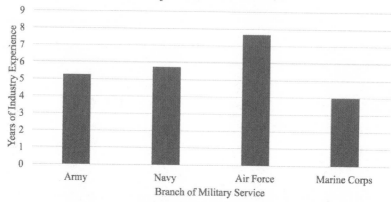

Industry Experience for Veterans at Goldman Sachs by Branch of Service

Figure 6 – Air Force Veterans have the most extensive amount of civilian work experience prior to joining Goldman Sachs.

Across all branches of service, the average Veteran has **6.2** years of civilian work experience prior to joining Goldman Sachs. This is heavily skewed by Air Force Veterans, who rack up an average of 7.7 years of civilian work experience prior to joining Goldman.

One last view of this data provides the most insight. Combining the two previous graphs, let's look at the combined work experience - both military and civilian – for a Veteran at Goldman Sachs who goes directly from industry to Goldman.

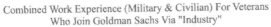

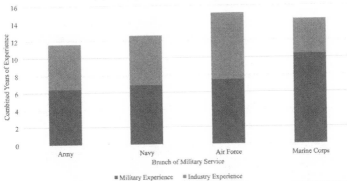

Figure 7 – The average Veteran at Goldman Sachs who works in industry prior to joining, has 13.4 years of combined military and civilian work experience
(For a color version of this chart, please visit BeyondTheUniform.io/goldman-charts)

Across all branches of service, for a Veteran taking the "industry" route to Goldman, they have **13.4** years of experience. Air Force and Marine Corps Veterans skew towards more experience, while Army and Navy Veterans skew towards less experience.

On final observation that I would like to make here. In looking at those Veterans who go to school directly prior to Goldman, their average length of military service is **8.2** years. As we'll see shortly, the MBA is the most common degree pursued by Veterans in this path. Given that business schools are typically two years in duration, this means that the average Veteran coming from school gets to Goldman with just **10.2** years of combined military and school experience. All other things being equal, this means that they arrive at Goldman a full **3.2** years before Veterans coming from Industry. This obviously overlooks so many factors including work experience, life experience, salary earned, etc. However, from a strictly time perspective I did think it was worth noting.

Education obtained by Veterans at Goldman Sachs

An important aspect to consider in any career path is the level of education that will be required. So, the next aspect we will consider is the highest level of education achieved by Veterans currently working at Goldman Sachs.

Please note that some Veterans hold multiple advanced degrees. Also, some Veterans may have achieved their highest level of education while at the consulting company. However, given the demanding schedule associated with Goldman Sachs, I don't believe it is likely that the Veteran advanced his/her education while working there. Here's what I found.

Highest Level of Education for Veterans at Goldman Sachs

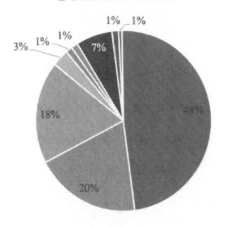

1% 1%
1% 1%
3% 1%
7%
48%
18%
20%

■ MBA ■ BS ■ BA ■ MA ■ PhD ■ JD ■ MS ■ Meng ■ MPM

Figure 8 – The most common degree for Veterans at Goldman
Sachs is an MBA
(For a color version of this chart, please visit
BeyondTheUniform.io/goldman-charts)

I found this refreshing. When I looked at the same data
for *Veterans in Consulting* I found that **89%** of Veterans
at The Big Three consulting firms had an MBA. For
Goldman, it is much more well-rounded. In fact, **38%** of
Veterans have either an BA or a BS. This is a great
aspect of working at Goldman Sachs. Between the
Veterans Integration Program and the on-the-job
training, you are likely to get all of the training you need,
and no advanced degree is required.

Given how many Veterans have an MBA, I wanted to provide a list of the most common schools for current Veterans at Goldman Sachs. These are the business schools I saw in my research:

1. University of Pennsylvania - The Wharton School
2. Duke University - The Fuqua School of Business
3. Columbia University - Columbia Business School
4. The University of Texas at Austin - Red McCombs School of Business
5. University of Southern California - Marshall School of Business
6. Harvard Business School
7. University of Washington, Michael G. Foster School of Business
8. University of North Carolina at Chapel Hill - Kenan-Flagler Business School
9. Rice University - Jesse H. Jones Graduate School of Business
10. Massachusetts Institute of Technology - Sloan School of Management
11. Northwestern University - Kellogg School of Management
12. University of Utah

It is important to recognize that the twelve schools listed above represent **51%** of the Veteran population at Goldman Sachs who have an MBA. This means that **49%** of Veterans obtain their MBA at another institution. Here again, my takeaway is that, while getting into Goldman Sachs is exceptionally difficult, there are many ways to gain entry into Goldman Sachs.

One final aspect about education I wanted to consider is what schools Veterans attend immediately prior to joining Goldman Sachs. Specifically, this looks at the "School" route and which MBA programs led to Goldman. Here's what I found:

MBA Programs Attended by Veterans Going Directly from School to Goldman Sachs

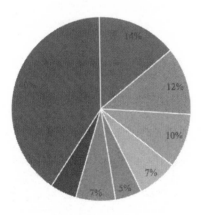

- University of Pennsylvania - The Wharton School
- Columbia University - Columbia Business School
- University of Southern California - Marshall School of Business
- University of North Carolina at Chapel Hill - Kenan-Flagler Business School
- Duke University - The Fuqua School of Business
- The University of Texas at Austin - Red McCombs School of Business
- Harvard Business School
- Other

Figure 9 – For Veterans going directly from school to Goldman Sachs, the most common Business School is the Wharton School (For a color version of this chart, please visit BeyondTheUniform.io/goldman-charts)

Here again, the largest portion of Veterans comes from Wharton (nearly one out of every seven Veterans in this path). However, with **40%** of Veterans coming from other schools, there is a wide range of business schools to choose from if this is your intended route.

So far, we have analyzed the first portion of data regarding the backgrounds of those Veterans working at Goldman Sachs. Next, we will look at trends at the most common titles held by Veterans, and their corresponding salary and job descriptions.

Titles & Salaries of Veterans at Goldman Sachs

The last two factors I considered were the most common job titles and their corresponding salaries for Veterans at Goldman Sachs, according to Glassdoor. I looked at total compensation (base salary and all bonuses), and used Glassdoor salary information using New York as the location for salary comparison.

One quick disclaimer: there are so many factors to consider when selecting a job – location, responsibilities, cultural fit, opportunity for advancement, etc. Salary is one of the easiest to quantify, but is not the most important factor to consider. My intention in delving into this data was merely to provide Veterans with more information so that they can make a decision that is right for them.

Let's start off by looking at the most common titles for Veterans at Goldman Sachs, and their corresponding estimated salary:

1. Associate (**28%** of Veterans at Goldman Sachs) – Total annual compensation estimated at $132,000

2. Vice President (**25%** of Veterans at Goldman Sachs) – Total annual compensation estimated at $217,000
3. Analyst (**13%** of Veterans at Goldman Sachs) – Total annual compensation estimated at - $88,000
4. Investment Management Division (**7%** of Veterans at Goldman Sachs) – Total annual compensation estimated at $128,500
5. Private Wealth Advisor (**5%** of Veterans at Goldman Sachs) – Total annual compensation estimated at $165,000
6. Managing Director (**4%** of Veterans at Goldman Sachs) – Total annual compensation estimated at $641,000

I want to reiterate a point I made in the Introduction chapter. The more senior Veterans at Goldman Sachs tend to list only one job, which corresponds to their current title. However, I am unaware of any Veteran (or non-Veteran) who enters into a title of Managing Director or Vice President. My assumption is that these Veterans started significantly more junior, and worked their way to this position over a long career. The most common entry-level titles correspond to Associate, Analyst, and Private Wealth Advisor.

As a result, I will provide some data about each of these six positions, and what you can learn about how Veterans achieve each of these roles.

Routes that Veterans take from the military to each job title

Let's look at the path a Veteran takes to obtain each of these six titles:

Veterans Path to Goldman Sachs for Associates

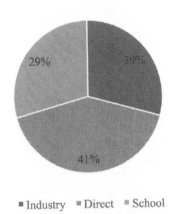

■ Industry ■ Direct ■ School

Figure 10 – Most Veterans at Goldman Sachs with the title of
Associate transition directly from the military to this role.
(For a color version of this chart, please visit
BeyondTheUniform.io/goldman-charts)

Veteran Paths to Goldman Sachs for Vice Presidents

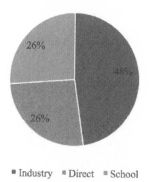

■ Industry ■ Direct ■ School

Figure 11 – Most Veterans at Goldman Sachs with the title of Vice President work in another job prior to this role.

Veterans Path to Goldman Sachs for Analyst

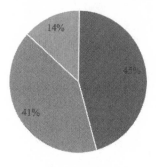

■ Industry ■ Direct ■ School

Figure 12 – A nearly equal number of Veterans at Goldman Sachs with the title of Analyst work in another job prior to this role, or transition directly from Active Duty.

Veterans Path to Goldman Sachs for Private
Wealth Advisor

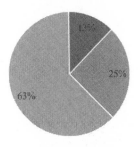

■ Industry ■ Direct ■ School

Figure 13 – The majority of Veterans at Goldman Sachs with the
title of Private Wealth Advisor went directly from school to this
role.

Veterans Path to Goldman Sachs for
Investment Management Division

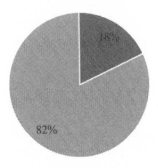

■ Industry ■ Direct ■ School

Figure 14 – The majority of Veterans at Goldman Sachs with the
title of Investment Management Division went directly from school
to this role.

Veterans Path to Goldman Sachs for Managing Director

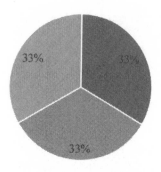

■ Industry   ■ Direct   ■ School

Figure 15 – The path to Managing Director at Goldman Sachs is equitably split between Industry, Direct, and School.

What to take away from all of this? Well, here are a few things that stood out to me. First of all, Analysts and Associates positions at Goldman Sachs are very appealing positions. **41%** of Veterans go directly from Active Duty to this role. Rather than transitioning from the military to school and spending time and money on an education, you can instead get paid in an extremely high-paced learning environment. To me, that is a very appealing prospect.

Second, the Private Wealth Management and Investment Management Division positions are similar in their trend to attract Veterans directly from school. If your aspiration is to join Goldman in one of these roles, it may be worth investigating going to school once you leave the military.

Third, the two more senior positions of Managing Director and Vice President both have fairly equitable paths. Each of these is fairly evenly distributed between the Direct, Industry, and School path.

Most common degrees for each job title

Next, let's take a look at the highest level of education a Veteran has in each of these roles. This could be a degree that the Veteran obtained immediately prior to joining Goldman, or it could be a degree they obtained while in the military. The goal is to provide insight into what level of education may be helpful when applying to these positions.

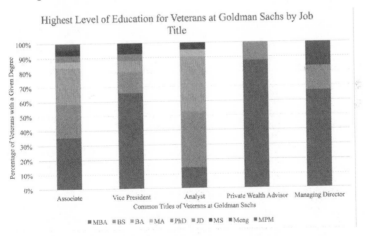

Figure 16 – The highest level of education achieved for Veterans at Goldman Sachs for the most popular job titles

(For a color version of this chart, please visit
BeyondTheUniform.io/goldman-charts)

There is quite a bit of information here. Let's distill this to the key insights that stood out to me. First of all, the Analyst position at Goldman Sachs is a terrific entry-level position. **41%** of Veterans in this role went directly from Active Duty to this position. And **76%** of these Veterans only have an undergraduate degree. For those desiring to make a quick transition without any additional education, Analyst is a solid starting point.

Second, the Associate position also seems to be a very good entry-level position. **41%** of Veterans in this role obtained it immediately after their Active Duty service. And **48%** of these Veterans only have an undergraduate degree. While this is markedly lower than that of an Analyst, it is still a relatively low barrier to application. It's also worth noting that over one-third of Associates do have an MBA. Given that only **29%** of Associates transition to Goldman from school, this leads me to believe that many Associates obtain their MBA while on Active Duty.

Third, for the higher-salaried positions of Private Wealth Advisor, Vice President, and Managing Director an MBA is more common than not. **88%** of all Private Wealth Advisors have an MBA, and **66%** and **67%** of Vice Presidents and Managing Directors, respectively, have an MBA as well. I interpret this that an MBA opens up more opportunity for career advancement within Goldman Sachs.

How branch of military service varies by job title

The final aspect I wanted to consider was how branch of service affects job title. Here's what I found:

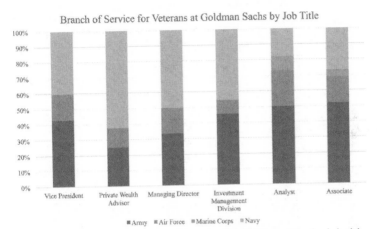

Figure 17 – A look at branch of service by Goldman Sachs job title (For a color version of this chart, please visit BeyondTheUniform.io/goldman-charts)

I feel obliged to say, one last time, that I believe branch of service provides the least insight on career path. That's said, here are some aspects that stand out to me.

The first is that Marines are represented in many positions at Goldman Sachs. Yet, in these select top six titles they are only represented in the Associate and Analyst positions. I look forward to revisiting this data in a few years, and fully expect to see Marines to have progressed to more senior positions within Goldman (again, this data is just a snapshot at this point in time).

Second, Private Wealth Advisor has an interesting characteristic. Army Veterans are the largest military representative for most roles at Goldman Sachs. However, for Private Wealth Advisors they comprise only **25%** of Veterans in this position. Navy Veterans, on the other hand, are overly represented here with **63%** of the Private Wealth Advisor positions.

At this point we have covered every aspect I could think of for Veterans at Goldman Sachs. So, let's bring this all home with some final, parting thoughts.

Conclusion

It can be extremely intimidating to select your first civilian career after serving in the military on Active Duty. I know that I was daunted by this transition, and I know that every single one of the 150+ Veterans I interviewed for *Beyond the Uniform* were intimidated by this as well.

I hope that this book has helped you better understand what a career at Goldman Sachs looks like, and has given you some initial indications of whether or not this would be a good career option for you. If it is, I hope it has given you the confidence to know that – should you set your sites on Goldman Sachs – **there is a clear path to get there and many Veterans are willing to help you along the way.**

One final story that I'll share is a lesson I learned five years after graduating from the Stanford Graduate School of Business. I – and each of my classmates at Stanford – spent hundreds of hours preparing our business school applications. We researched the career we wanted to pursue after business school, and wrote convincing essays speaking to our conviction about that career path. Then, once we got to business school, we changed our minds about our desired career, threw it out the window, and started researching a new career option! We furiously prepared for our summer internship interviews, once again convinced that we had figured out what we wanted to do.

Then, we went off to our summer internships, and over the course of ten-weeks, I – and, again, the overwhelming majority of my classmates – realized that we had gotten our ideal career wrong. So, we spent the majority of our second year at business school researching, identifying, and preparing for our first job out of business school. One year out of business school, the majority of my classmates had started a second job. Two years, the majority of my classmates were heading in another direction as well. At this point, nine years out from business school, a month doesn't go by where I talk with a classmate who is considering shifting their career!

I'm not sharing this story to intimidate you, but rather the opposite – to let you know that this is part of the process. If you start your civilian career and believe it is the end-all-be-all, it's highly likely that you're going to be disappointed when, at some point, you shift to a different career. However, if you approach looking at a career at Goldman Sachs (or even if you approach starting your career in finance) as merely the first of many "lily pads" on your way to your ideal career path, I believe you'll be more realistic in your approach and more fulfilled in your results.

From the 150+ interviews I've done with military Veterans I have seen, time and time again, that Veterans can do whatever it is they would like to do in their civilian careers. While I do believe that Goldman Sachs is an exceptional company for many Veterans, I also know that each of us is different in our abilities, desires, and ambitions. I hope this book has served as a resource towards your finding your ideal career.

There is no one who deserves that more than those who have served our country so selflessly.

About the Author

Justin M. Nassiri is the Founder & CEO of StoryBox, and started *Beyond the Uniform* as a side project to help active duty military personnel. With *Beyond the Uniform*, he has conducted over 150 interviews with military Veterans about their civilian careers: what they do, how they got there, and their advice to other Veterans. He has had the privilege of interviewing the CEO of Pepsi, NFL players, Academy Award nominees, and more.

He started out United States Naval Academy, where he studied Electrical Engineering. He also received the world's finest education in leadership, serving as the Brigade Performance and Conduct Officer and the President of the Men's Glee Club. (As a result, his wife Rebecca refers to herself as the First Lady.)

After the Naval Academy, Justin served as an Officer with the incredible crew of the USS Alaska (SSBN 732) and for a far-too-brief time with the USS Chicago. This training was the single biggest asset to his experience as an entrepreneur, helping him break through walls, push himself beyond his limits, and occasionally fight giant squid as well as flirt with mermaids.

His life was forever changed when he attended the Stanford Graduate School of Business. There, he learned that investment bankers weren't tellers at a bank (true story), that ordinary people can start baby companies called startups, and that if you're dressed in 70s attire on a flight to Vegas, you can get away with giving the safety announcement.

He has worked as a Consultant with McKinsey & Company at their New York Office. He also founded StoryBox, a marketing technology company that has raised over $3M in venture capital, and worked with over 35 Fortune 500 companies including Disney, Budweiser, and Microsoft.

Justin lives in Denver, Colorado with the love of his life, Rebecca, and their strong-willed dog, Hemingway.

Made in the USA
Columbia, SC
31 October 2021